Triangles

ISBN-13: 978-1502817006
ISBN-10: 1502817004

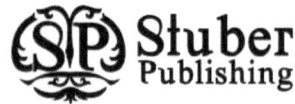

Stuber
Publishing

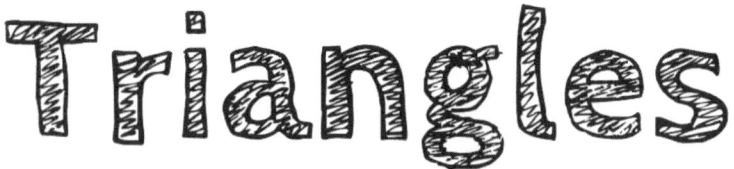

Triangles

Curated by Melissa Staiger

ventana244 GALLERY

Liz Ainslie

Li Trincere

Julie Weitz

Jon Cowan

Jason Rohlf

Mark Dagley

Ben LaRocco

Vincent Como

Brooke Moyse

Peter Acheson

Maria Hupfield

Elizabeth Hazan

DeShawn Dumas

RossanaMartinez

Osamu Kobayashi

Glen Cunningham

Janet Kurnatowski

Curatorial Statement – Melissa Staiger

The seventeen artists in *Triangles* incorporate the triangle shape through various painted and drawn layers, through the lens, being sewn and performed. It creates an environment where the viewer can reflect on the triangular form in its different manifestations.

As science and consciousness on our planet are expanding into new and unknown territory, the triangular shape reveals itself as a symbol that has been full of meaning ever since. The triangle serves as a building block of life in the tiniest particles of our universe, and for thousands of years many cultures have used it as a powerful symbol.

Wassily Kandinsky (1886 – 1944), the influential Russian abstract painter, followed a mystical tradition and created *Variegation in the Triangle* (1927), one of his most renowned pieces. He stated: "*Who knows, maybe all our 'abstract' forms are 'forms in nature'.*"

The Ukrainian-born painter and famous textile designer Sonja Delaunay (1885 – 1979) prolifically used the triangle shape in her clothing designs and paintings. She created the oil painting *Electric Prisms* (1913), which influenced her life's work.

Blinky Palermo's (1943 – 1977) *Triangle above a Door* (1969) is referenced in this exhibition. The blue triangle is painted above a doorway, and the German native believed it contained mystical powers. He also created a stencil DYI kit for patrons.

Triangles provides a contemporary interpretation and integration of the triangular form. The artists in the exhibition start a new discussion, right where Kandinsky, Delaunay and Palermo have left off. Following the theme, artists and writers Nadema Agard, Craig Olson and Stephen Westfall express what the Triangle shape means to them for a faceted experience.

Here followeth the Figure conteyning all the secrets of the Treatise both great and small

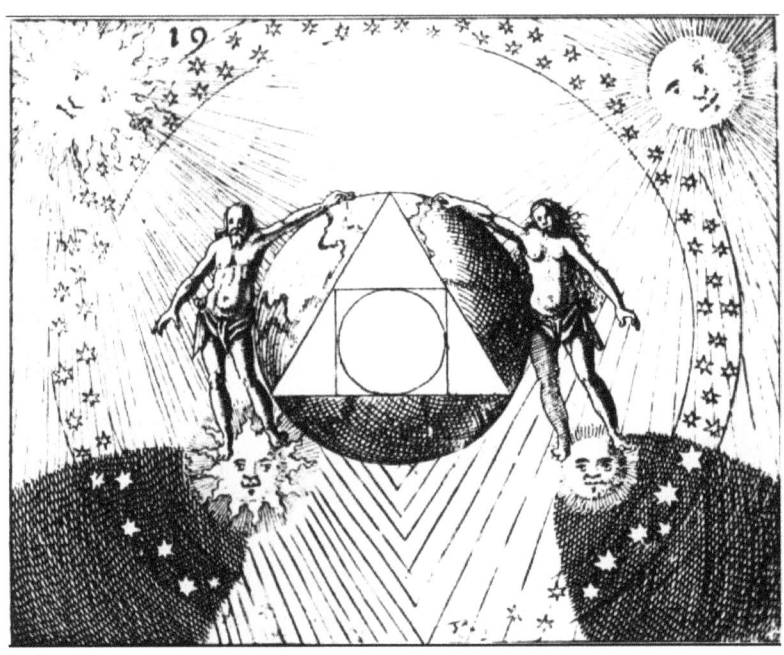

Image: D. Stolcius von Stolzenberg, *Viridarium Chymicum*, Frankfurt, 1624

On a fine spring evening, the lag lay dreaming
And the seagulls were wheeling high above the wall
And that auld triangle, went jingle jangle
All along the banks of the Royal Canal

-Ye Auld Triangle

"The Triangle (alchemical fire) acts to connect and integrate the above with the below. In the same way it signifies liberation from the confines of literalist duality. Extending outward from its inner psychic structure, human consciousness is brought into divine relationship with the cosmos, which in turn extends deeper into human consciousness. Thus, there is inner and outer harmony with oneself and the universe. But harmony has a shadow, just as all triads constellate their dark twin. Cut the square in half diagonally and you have two triads pointing in opposite directions.

This new triad born from the death of wholeness (the square) sits in diametric opposition to its twin. Dark and mysterious, lacking the blinding light of reason, it contains the silvery light of reflection. The inverted Triangle (alchemical water) is the flowing of the dark, nocturnal, lower elements. Thus, our correspondence is formed.

To strive for a unification of these principles is a fool's errand. For unity, as Jung reminds us, is not an empirical reality, not part of our lived world. It is the fantasy image of a goal. When trapped in the literalist prison of this goal, only the jingle jangle of ye auld triangle can connect us to the anima-like gulls soaring above. In the ringing of this third component, the multiplicity of self takes wing.

In such a state, the squabbling ideologies of Casualism and Liminalism, Anarchism and Libertarianism, Christianity and Atheism – all fantasies that long for a unifying separation from the tangled mess of here and now – atrophy into a single lump of vicious stupidity. All forms of determinism seem equally vapid – we're slaves of neither our genes, nor our machines, nor our ideologies. What is 'natural' is what we imagine & create."

Craig Olson, 2014

"I love triangles, partly because I love Euclid. They are the simplest shape we can make with straight lines. But I also love them because they can lock into a rectangle while simultaneously delivering animating angles. They are itchy and active. Draw any diagonal from a vertical side of rectangle through the top or bottom horizontal side and you immediately have a triangle. And that triangle may not be a triangle at all, but the edge of a much larger shape or area outside the frame. Triangles can thus be very ambiguous and I like, how should I put it, clear ambiguities.

They also have potential for morphing into more complex shapes: diamonds and increasingly complicated polygons. Symmetrical polygons can be corralled into grids. Of all the elemental shapes triangles have the broadest capacity for gesture: a single triangle can stand on point or reach for its pinnacle. It is the tense space they inhabit between order and disorder that makes them daemonic: always creating energy, a kind of wild magic."

Stephen Westfall, 2014

"In ancient times, women on the Northern Plains were the first abstract artists. They created earth paintings with natural pigments before any of the more commonly known traditional arts became known.

In this manner women produce beautifully painted 'Parfleche' bags made out of rawhide using geometric symbols, most commonly, triangles. For example two triangles like mirror images (in a form of an X) were often painted to convey esoteric knowledge in order to explain the universe in terms of dualities and mutual reciprocities."

Nadema Agard/*Winyan Luta*/Red Woman, 2014
(Cherokee/Lakota/Powhatan)

Peter Acheson

Peter Acheson (b. 1954) lives and works in Columbia County, New York, surrounded by farmland giving over to second homes. He practices painting and child raising, cloud and moon watching.

His work is a direct response to his environment, a result of his move from Brooklyn to upstate. He paints with no parameters or 'edges', but uses text and objects as poetry. Acheson was one of the original artists in the early Williamsburg art scene of the late 70's and 80's.

His recent solo exhibition "*Doormroom Paintings Part 1*" (2011) was shown at Stephen Harvey Fine Art Projects, and "*Rusted Giacometti*" (2014) at NOVELLA Gallery.

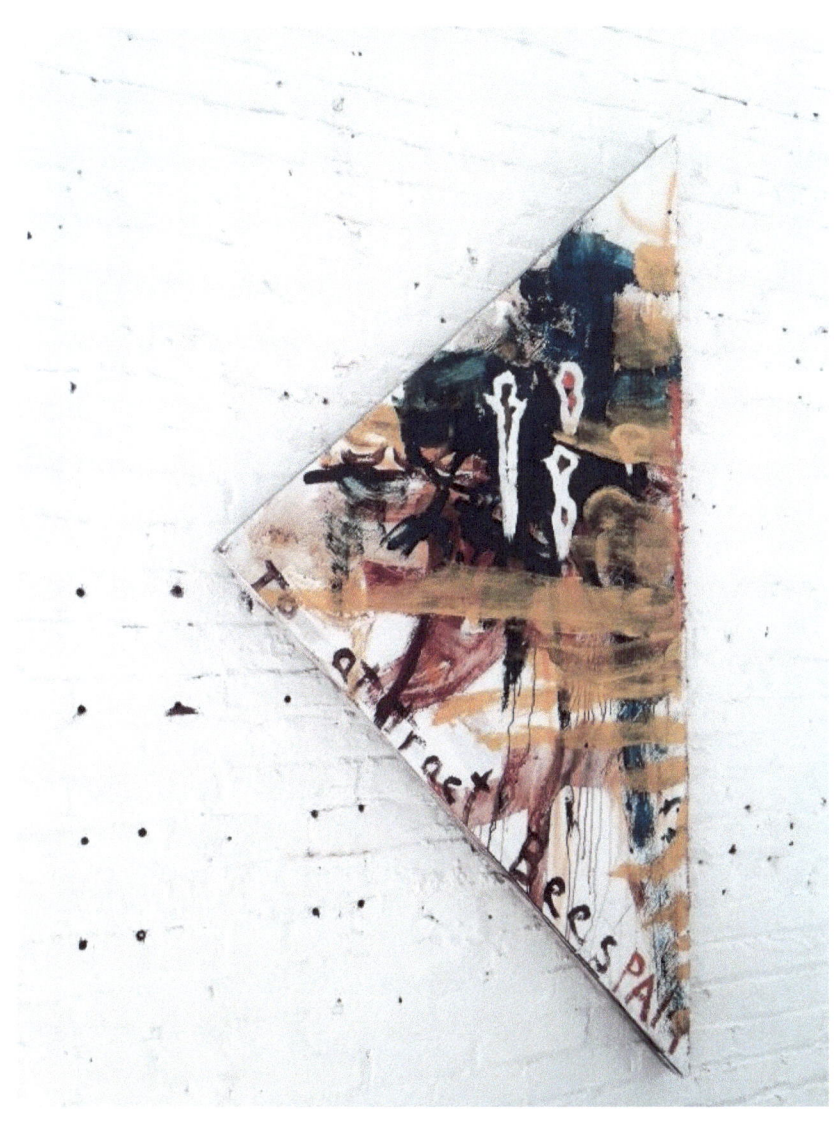

Attract Bees, acrylic on wood, 40 x 29 inches, 2014

Liz Ainslie

Liz Ainslie lives and works in Brooklyn, New York. She received her Master of Fine Arts from Tyler School of Art in 2004 and a Bachelor of Fine Arts from Alfred University in 2001. Ainslie has had solo shows at Airplane in Bushwick, Brooklyn and Creon Gallery in Manhattan.

Her work has been included in shows at Outlet Fine Art, Centotto, Parallel Art Space, Small Black Door, Sardine, 245 Varet, The Active Space, Norte Maar, A.M. Richard Fine Art, and A.I.R. gallery in Brooklyn; Valentine in Ridgewood, Queens; Lu Magnus, Artjail and Spazio 522 in Manhattan; Vox Populi and Ice Box Project Space in Philadelphia; BCB Fine Art and Imogen Holloway in upstate New York, and Gallerie Kritiku, Prague, Czech Republic.

Her work has been reviewed in *Giornale Dell' Arte, ArtCal Zine, The GC Advocate,* interviews with Ainslie can be found on a number of blogs including *And Freedom For, NYC Art Parasites, Pencil in the Studio, #ffffff Walls, Standard Interview, Otino Corsano,* and her paintings were featured on *Art Blog Art Blog, Ferse-Verse, and A/ART.* Her work can also be found in the Pierogi Flat Files. Ainslie was awarded residencies at Millay Colony for the Arts (2011) and Atlantic Center for the Arts (2006).

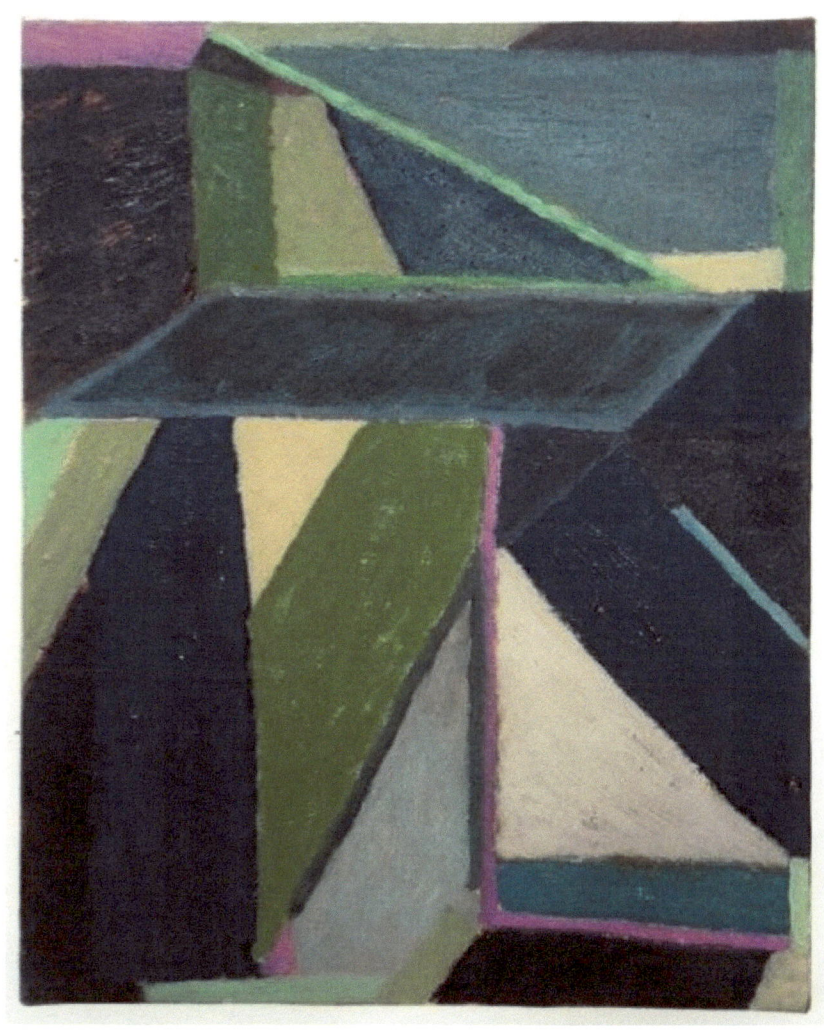

Think That Holds, oil on linen, 12 x 9 inches, 2014

Vincent Como

Vincent Como (b. 1975, Kittanning, Pennsylvania) lives Brooklyn, New York, and has exhibited his work throughout the United States and abroad, including Mexico, England, and Austria.

Recent solo and group exhibitions include MINUS SPACE, Art in General, BRIC Rotunda Gallery, Momenta (all New York City); Samson Projects (Boston, Massachusetts); Illinois State Museum (Lockport, Illinois); Western Exhibitions, University of Illinois (both Chicago, Illinois); Evanston Art Center (Evanston, Illinois); SPACES (Cleveland, Ohio); Urban Institute for Contemporary Arts (Grand Rapids, Michigan); Art Museum of the University of Memphis (Memphis, Tennessee); and House Gallery (Salt Lake City, Utah), among many others.

Como's work has been discussed in publications, such as *The Wall Street Journal, New American Paintings Blog, ArtSlant, Progress Report, WagMag, The Boston Phoenix, Chicago Tribune, Chicago Journal,* and *Salt Lake Tribune*, among others. He holds a Bachelor of Fine Arts in Drawing from the Cleveland Institute of Art, Ohio.

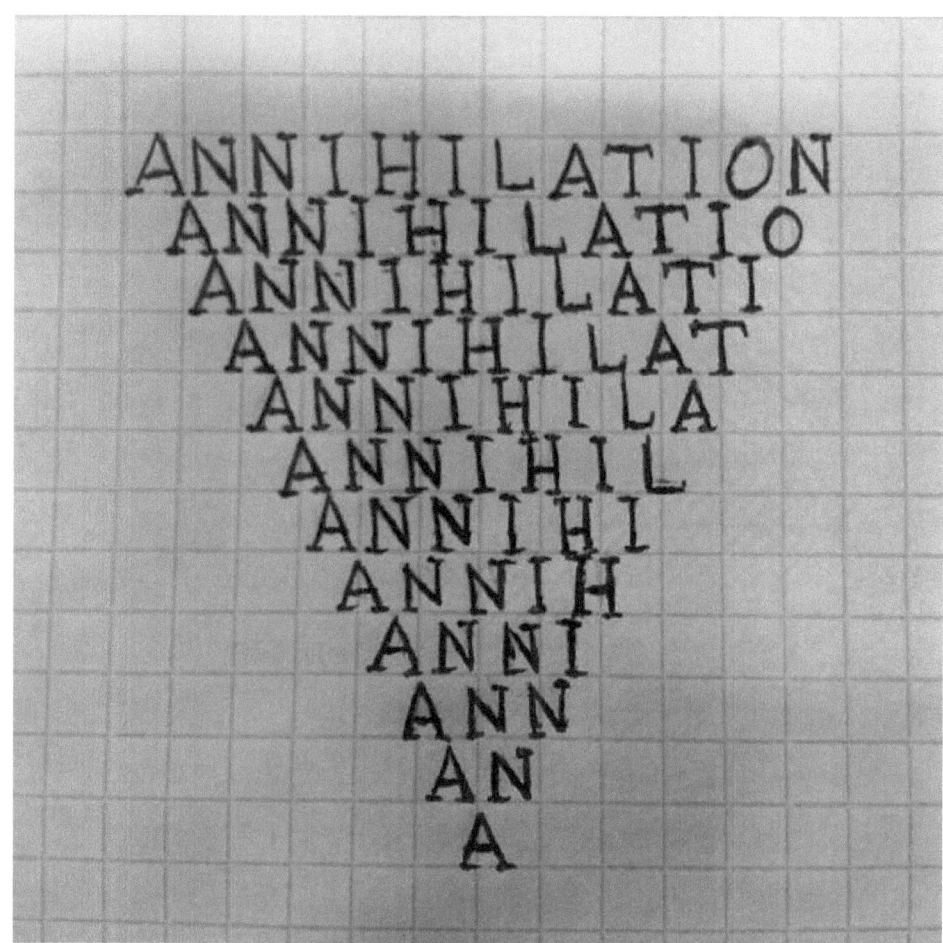

Prayer, pen on paper, 8.5 x 11 inches, 2012

Jon Cowan

Jonathan Cowan (b. 1982, Temple, Texas) attended The University of Texas at San Antonio where he received his Bachelor of Fine Arts in Drawing in 2006. **He lives and works in New York City.**

Cowan had a solo exhibition in 2014 titled, "*A Holy Mountain*" at 325 St Nicholas, New York City.

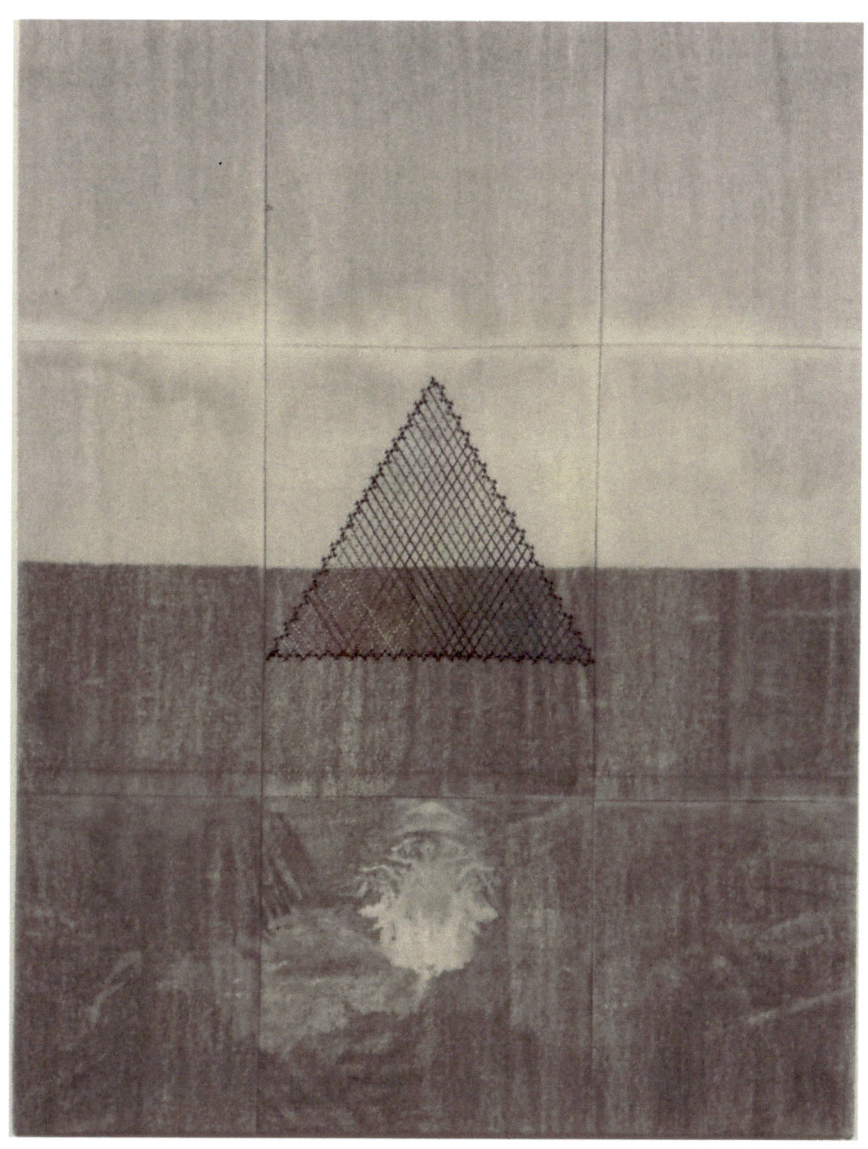

Black Ocean, transfer and embroidery on canvas, 18 x 24 inches, 2014

Glen Cunningham

Glen Cunningham was born and raised in New Orleans, Louisiana, and received his Bachelor of Fine Arts from Loyola University, Louisiana, in 1998. In the summer of 2001, he moved to Brooklyn, New York, to study at Pratt Institute, where he received his Master of Fine Arts in 2004.

He remembers being taught the compositional theories of the Renaissance painter Raphael, where a diagram of his "*Madonna and Child*" illustrated how a triangular composition was structurally strong. In the diagram, the figures were reduced to minimal formal shapes. It was further explained how the viewers' eyes would unconsciously follow this triangular composition.

The movement of someone's eyes following the forms and lines in a painting truly interests him, and the visual flow and movement of composition has since become an important aspect of his work. Cunningham also takes inspiration from architecture, geometry, astronomy, and construction. He lives and works in Brooklyn.

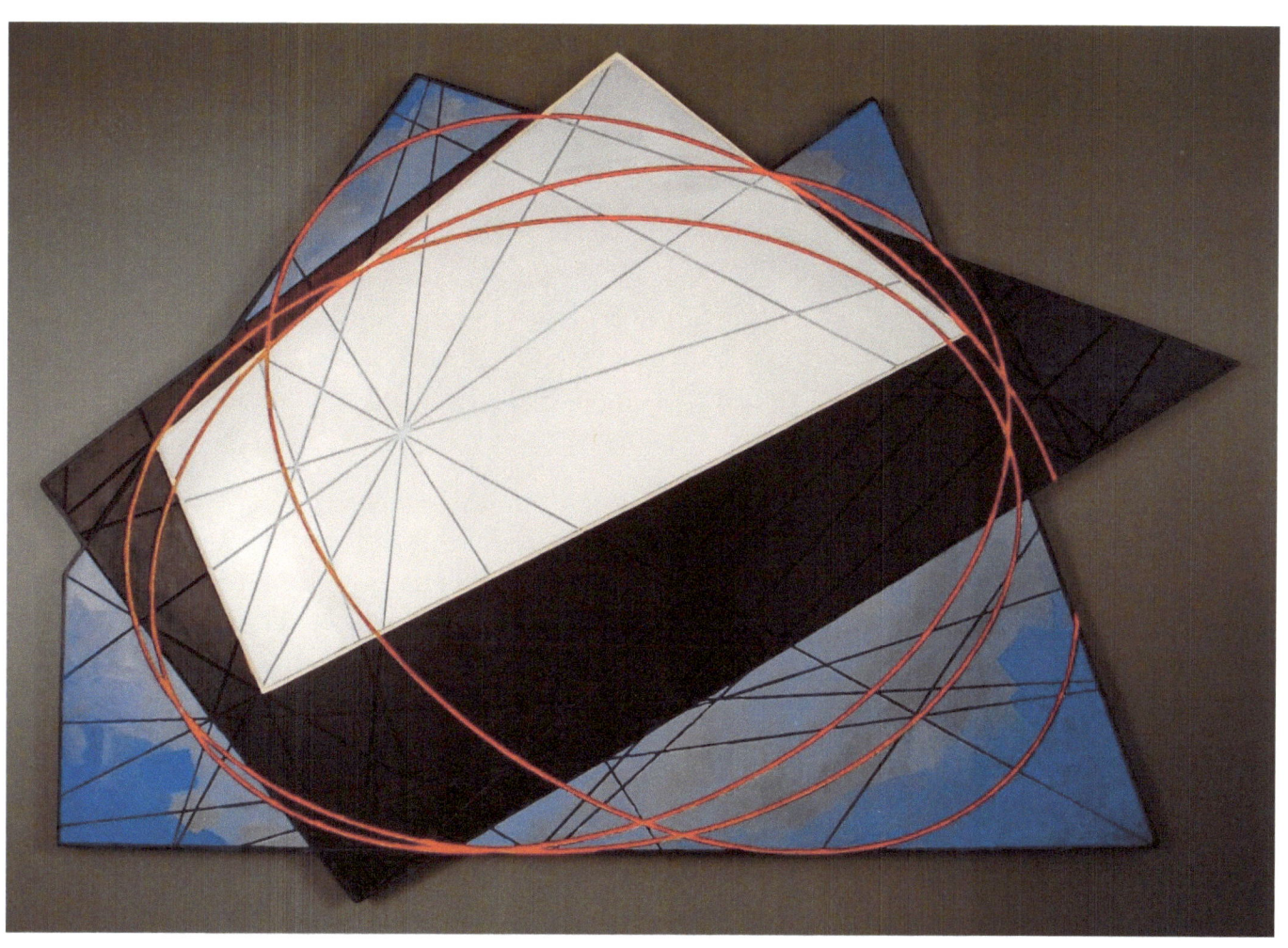

Movement of Three, oil and acrylic on shaped birch plywood, 35 x 50 inches, 2014

Mark Dagley

Mark Dagley (b. 1957, Washington, DC) has exhibited his work internationally for the past three decades, including in North America, Europe, and Australasia. During the 1980s, he was active in the East Village abstract painting scene and showed alongside other pioneering abstract painters, including Barry X Ball, Max Gimblett, Olivier Mosset, James Nares, Stephen Parrino, Li Trincere, and Alan Uglow, among many others.

Dagley's work was included in the groundbreaking group exhibition *Post-Hypnotic*, which traveled throughout the United States from 1999-2001. His work *Concentric Sequence* (1996) was featured on the cover of the exhibition catalog. During his career, Dagley has worked with a number of influential galleries worldwide, including Tony Shafrazi Gallery (New York City), Galerie Hans Strelow (Dusseldorf, Germany), Galeria Mar Estrada (Madrid, Spain), and Galerie Swart (Amsterdam, The Netherlands).

Dagley is a member of American Abstract Artists and his work has been reviewed in publications, such as *Artforum, Art in America, Flash Art International, The Brooklyn Rail, Artnet Magazine,* and *Time Out New York*. His work is included in the collections of Museo Nacional Centro de Arte Reina Sofia, Musee des beaux-arts de La Chaux-de-Fonds, Kunstmuseum St. Gallen, Swiss Credit Union, Foundation Prini, Hoffman/LaRoche, Henkel GmbH, EMI Madrid, Bloomingdale's Corporation, and the University of Michigan Museums of Art.

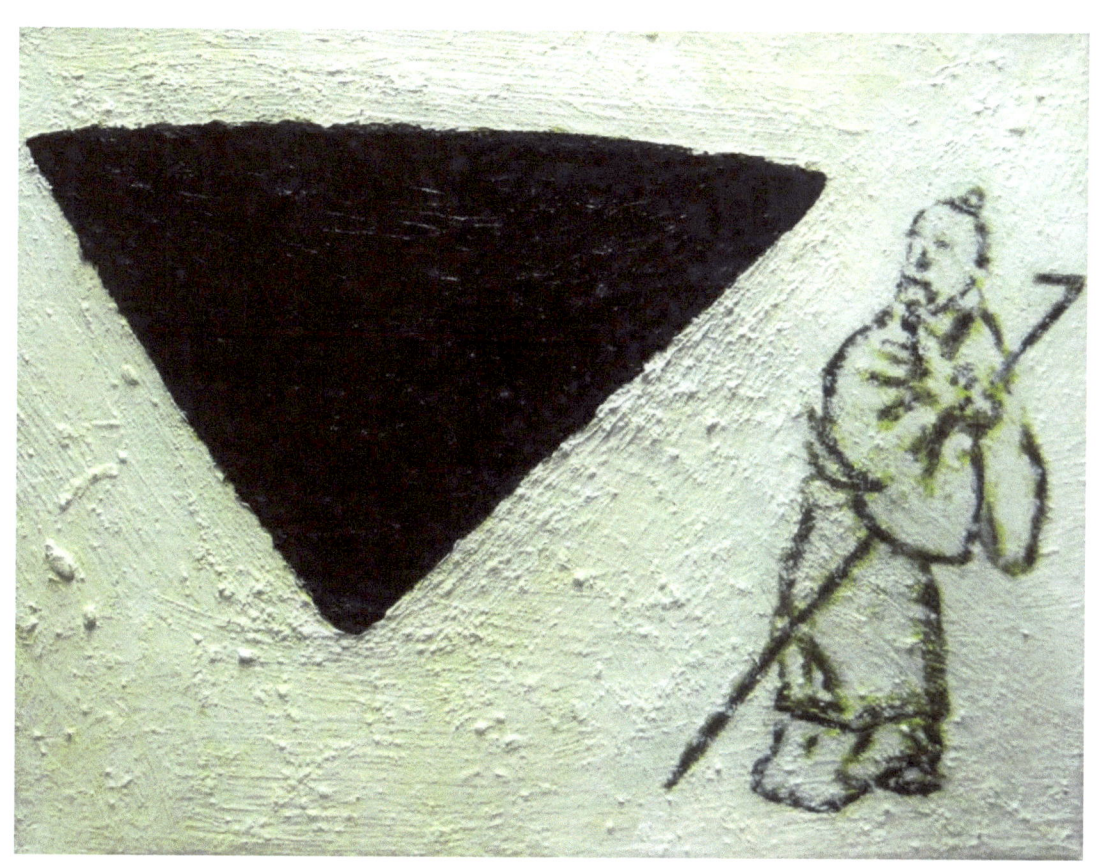

Dark Enlightenment, oil on linen, 8 x 10 inches, 2013

DeShawn Dumas

DeShawn Dumas is a Brooklyn, New York, based painter who works with a variety of material. He is a fellow of Pratt Institute, Brooklyn, and received a Master of Fine Arts in 2013 and a Master of Art and Design in 2014. In 2015, he will attend Tisch School of the Arts at New York University, in pursuit of a Ph.D. in Performance Studies.

In 2013, he had a solo exhibition titled "*Future Primitive*" at Janet Kurnatowski Gallery, Brooklyn.

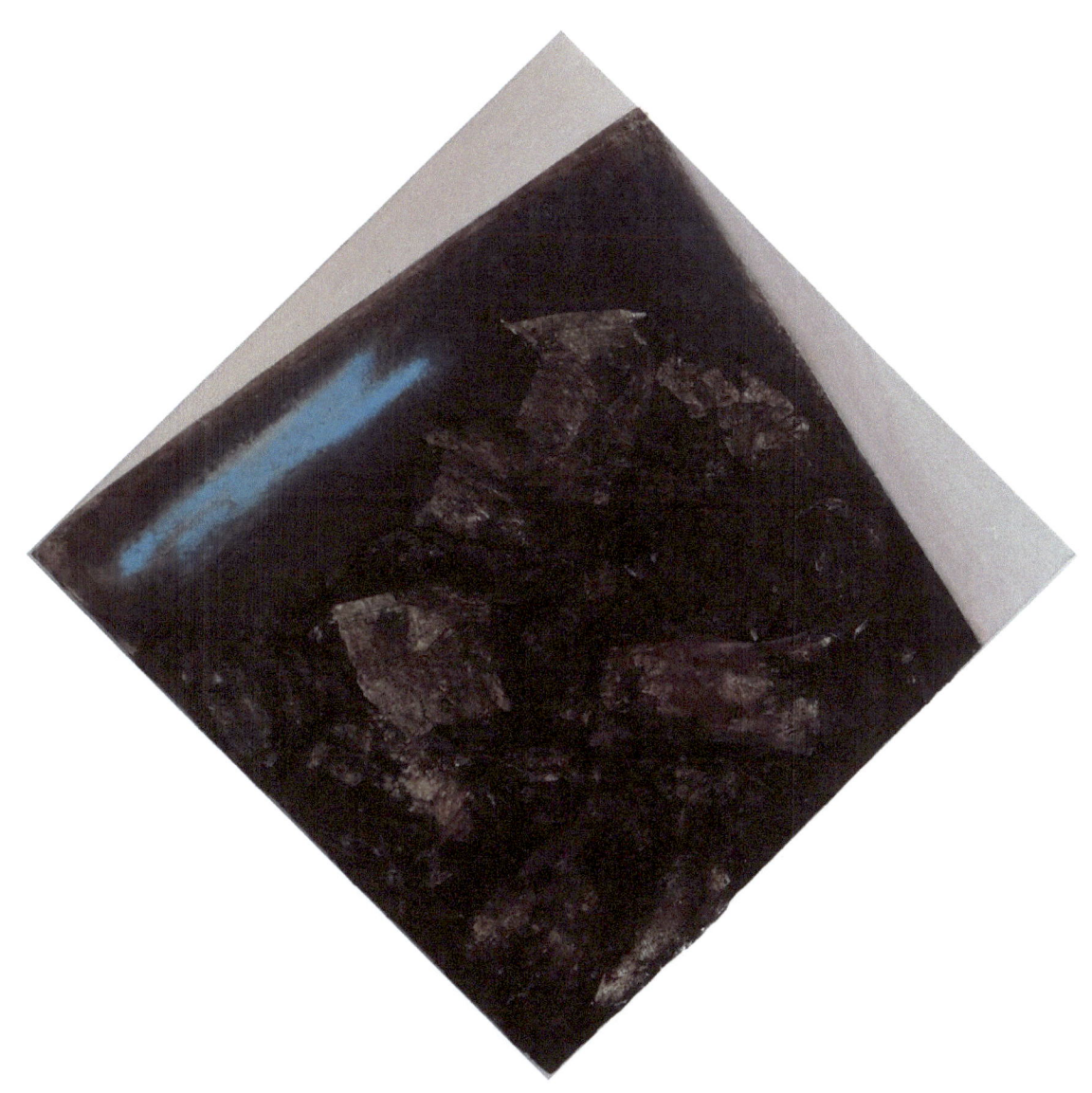

Dream of it (earth, death, rage), pages of the Book of Revelations,
coffee grinds, tar, oil, on canvas, 34 x 34 x 1 inches, 2012

Elizabeth Hazan

Elizabeth Hazan is an abstract artist who was born and raised in New York City. She attended the New York Studio School, where she received a fellowship to Skowhegan School of Painting and Sculpture and more recently was a resident of artist residency Yaddo.

She has exhibited in galleries and museums throughout the United States and is represented by Janet Kurnatowski Gallery, Brooklyn. She is the co-curator of an exhibition which features artists who use collage in their practice.

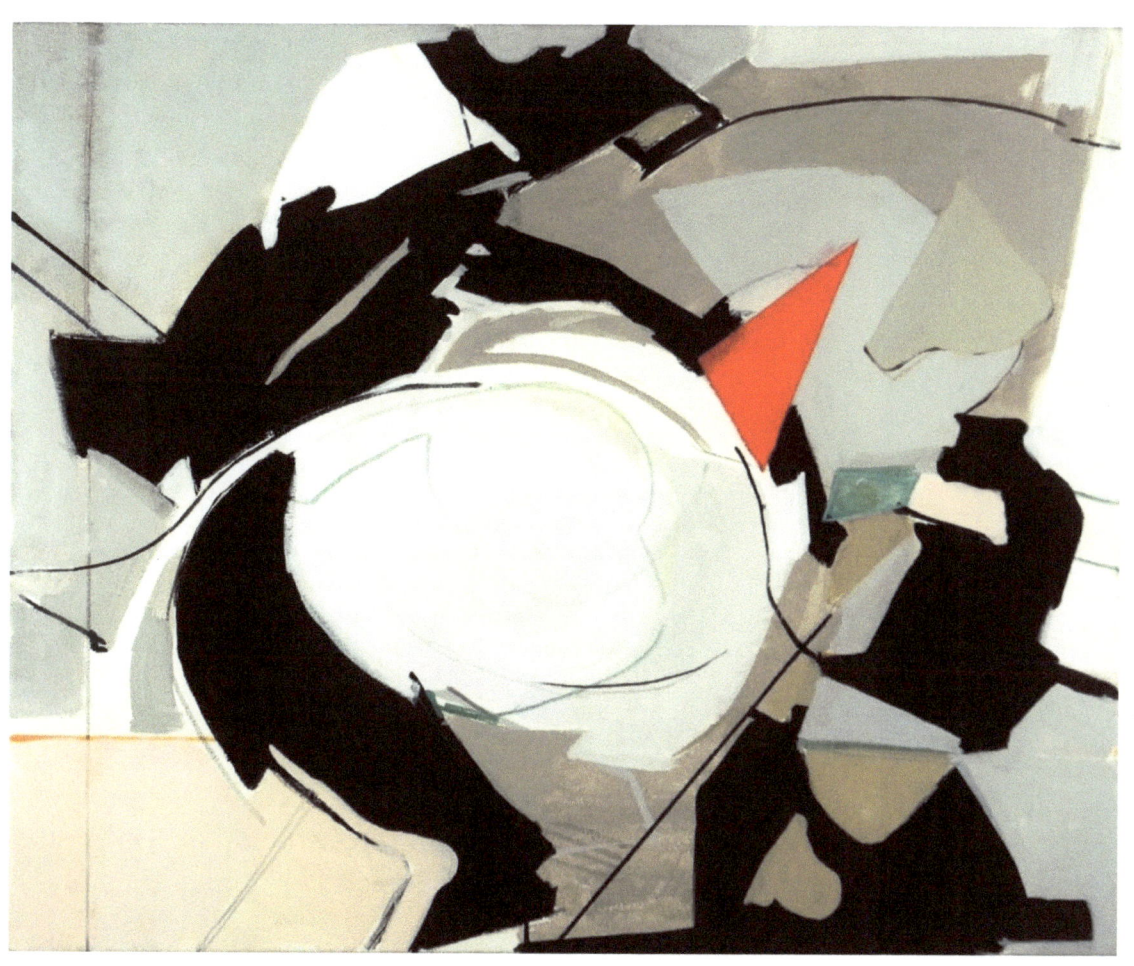

Current Weather, dispersed pigment on canvas, 20 x 24 inches, 2014

Maria Hupfield

Maria Hupfield (b. 1975, Parry Sound, Ontario) is from Canada, based in Brooklyn, New York, and a member of Wasauksing First Nation, Ontario. She is a 2014 recipient of the Joan Mitchell Foundation Painting and Sculpture Grant, the AIM residency at the Bronx Museum and a member of the Social Health Performance Club, Panoply Performance Lab.

Her work has traveled to the Museum of Arts and Design New York with the exhibition *Changing Hands III* and *The Power Plant Toronto for Beat Nation: Art, Hip Hop and Aboriginal Culture*. Maria is represented by Galerie Hugues Charbonneau, Montreal, Canada.

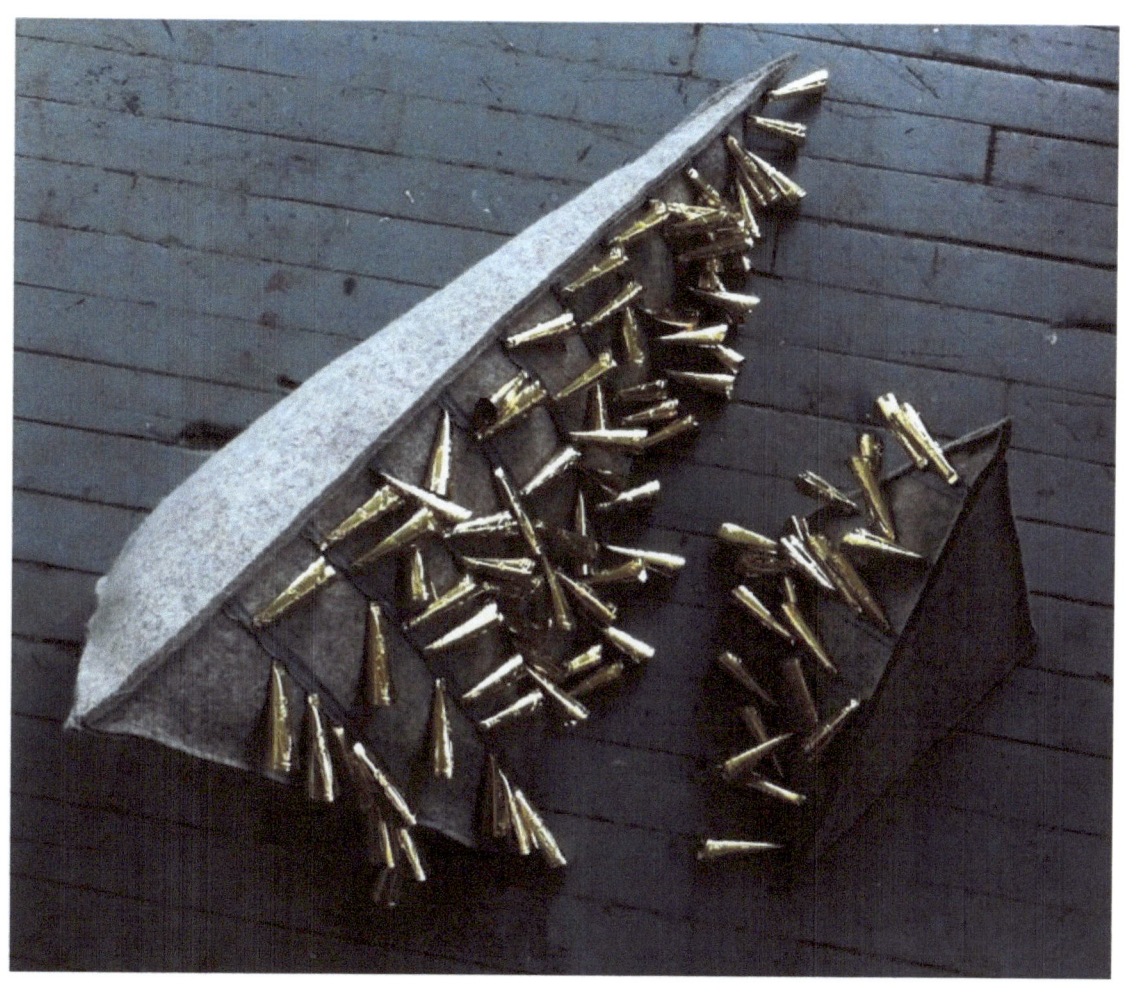

Triangle I and II, felt, polyfill, cotton thread, jingles, 13 x 17 x 33 and 9 x 11 x 16 inches, 2014

Osamu Kobayashi

Osamu Kobayashi (b. 1984, Columbia, South Carolina) lives and works in Brooklyn, New York. He has exhibited widely in the United States and abroad including solo exhibitions at the Greenwich House in New York City, AplusB Contemporary Art in Italy, and John Davis Gallery in New York City.

He was been awarded the Hassam, Speicher, Betts, and Symons Purchase Fund from the American Academy of Arts and Letters and is a recipient of the Morris Louis '32 scholarship.

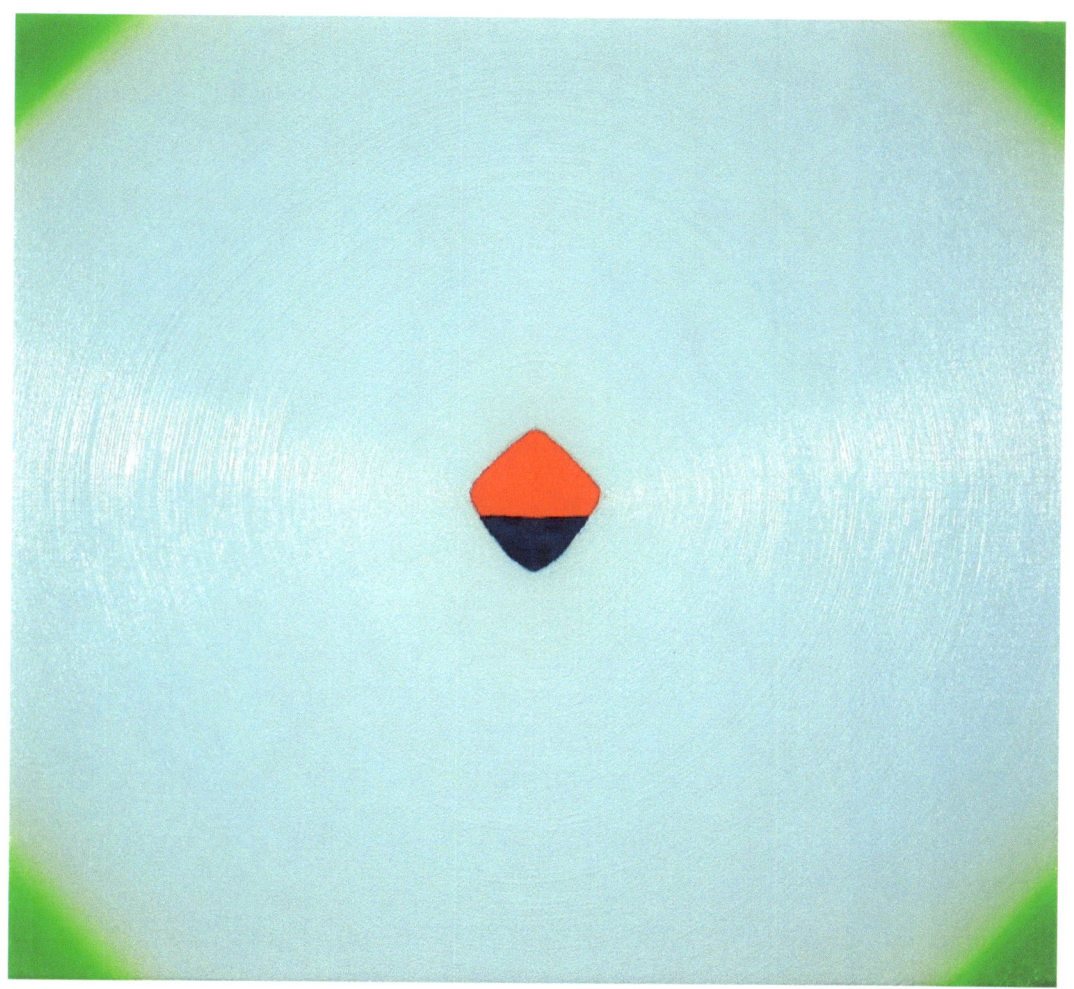

Frog See Sea, oil on linen, 11 x 12 inches, 2014

Janet Kurnatowski

Janet Kurnatowski (b. 1978) lives and works in Brooklyn, New York. She received her Bachelor of Business Management from Hofstra University and a Master of Fine Arts from Pratt Institute, Brooklyn. She is a sculptor who also paints, a professional makeup artist, jewelry designer and gallerist. In 2014, she celebrated the 10th anniversary of her gallery.

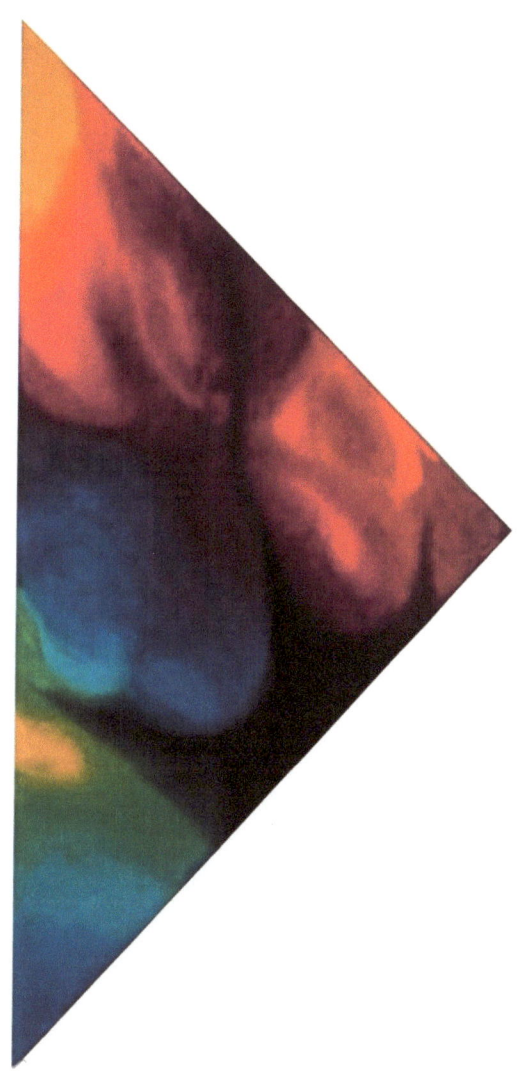

Darkness Within, oil on canvas, 9 x 8.75 x 2.75 inches, 2013

**Ben
La Rocco's**
house in Brooklyn
fell down last night. And
every part of it vanished into the
earth around him and his family. In
the night, before anyone awoke, he rebuilt it
exactly as it was, every brick and beam. And there
it stands ——— proof of the probability of the impossible.

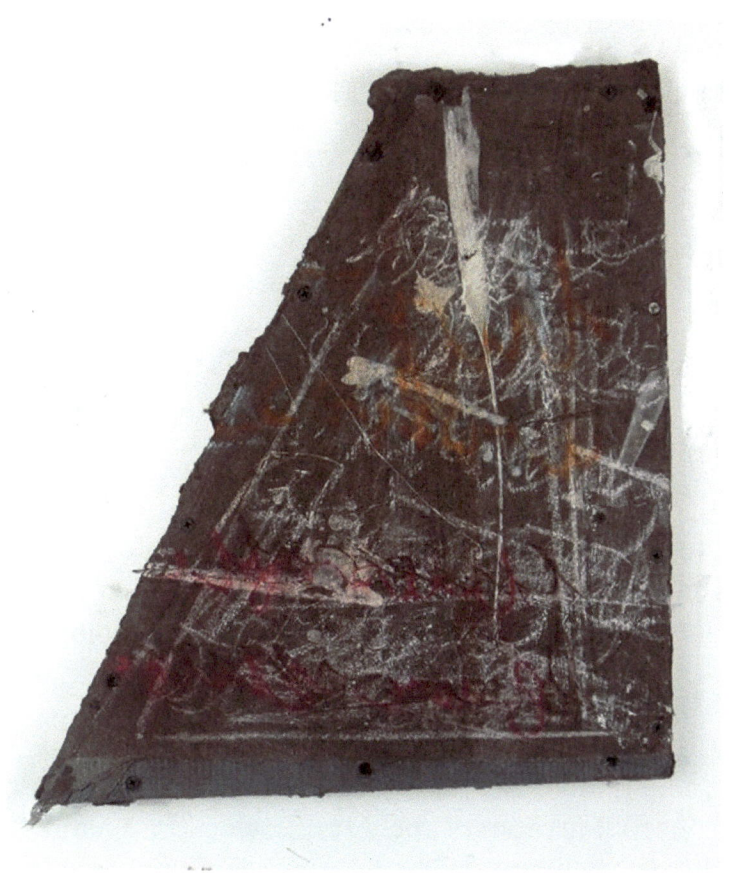

For Melissa, mixed media on masonite, dimensions vary 18 x 14 inches, 2014

Rossana Martinez

Rossana Martinez is an artist interested in conceptual and performance art. Her work investigates subtleties of balance and movement, which is based on her running and yoga practice. Rossana was born and raised in Puerto Rico, and holds a Master of Fine Arts in Sculpture and Printmaking from Pratt Institute, Brooklyn, New York, and a Bachelor of Liberal Arts from the University of Puerto Rico.

Her work has been exhibited nationally and internationally. She has received awards from the Brooklyn Arts Council, Bronx Museum of the Arts, Lower Manhattan Cultural Council, and El Diario La Prensa. Her work has been reviewed in publications, such as *The New York Times, The Village Voice, The Brooklyn Rail* and *Flavorpill*. In 2003, Rossana founded and currently directs MINUS SPACE, a gallery for abstract/reductive art based in Brooklyn.

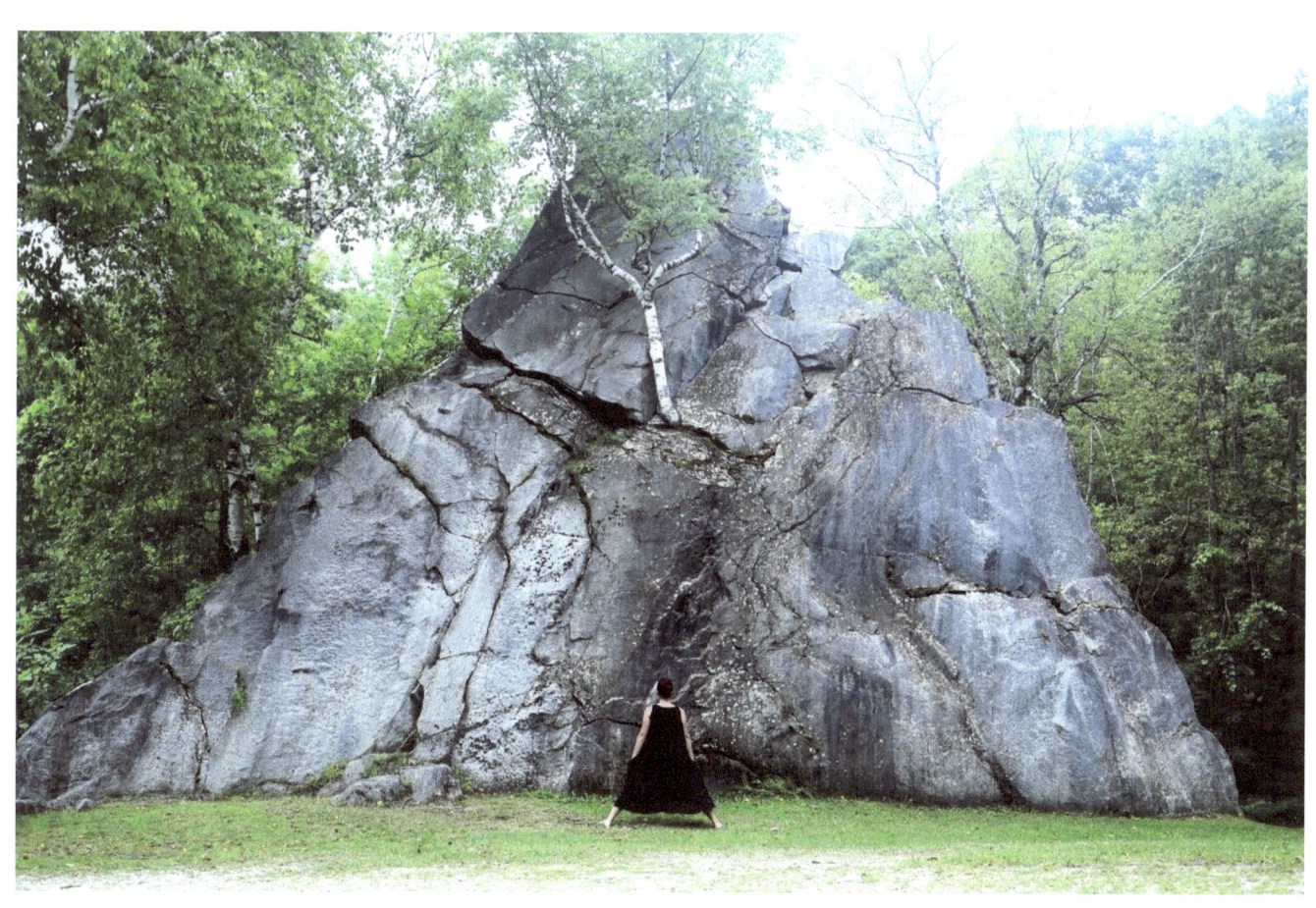

Body Geometry (Take Me To That Other Place), one-person performance with mountain, archival pigment print, 9.25 x 14 inches, edition of 5, 2014

Brooke Moyse

Brooke Moyse lives and works in Brooklyn, New York. She makes abstract paintings and drawings of geometric forms. The works vary in size while maintaining a looseness of composition and intimacy of touch, paired with a bold color sensibility.

Moyse received a Master of Fine Arts from New York University and a Bachelors degree from Bard College. She has exhibited at Tiger Strikes Asteroid in Philadelphia, David Klein Gallery in Bloomfield Hills, Michigan, Sundaram Tagore Gallery in Singapore, and at Storefront, Norte Maar, Momenta art and Loretta Howard Gallery among others, in New York.

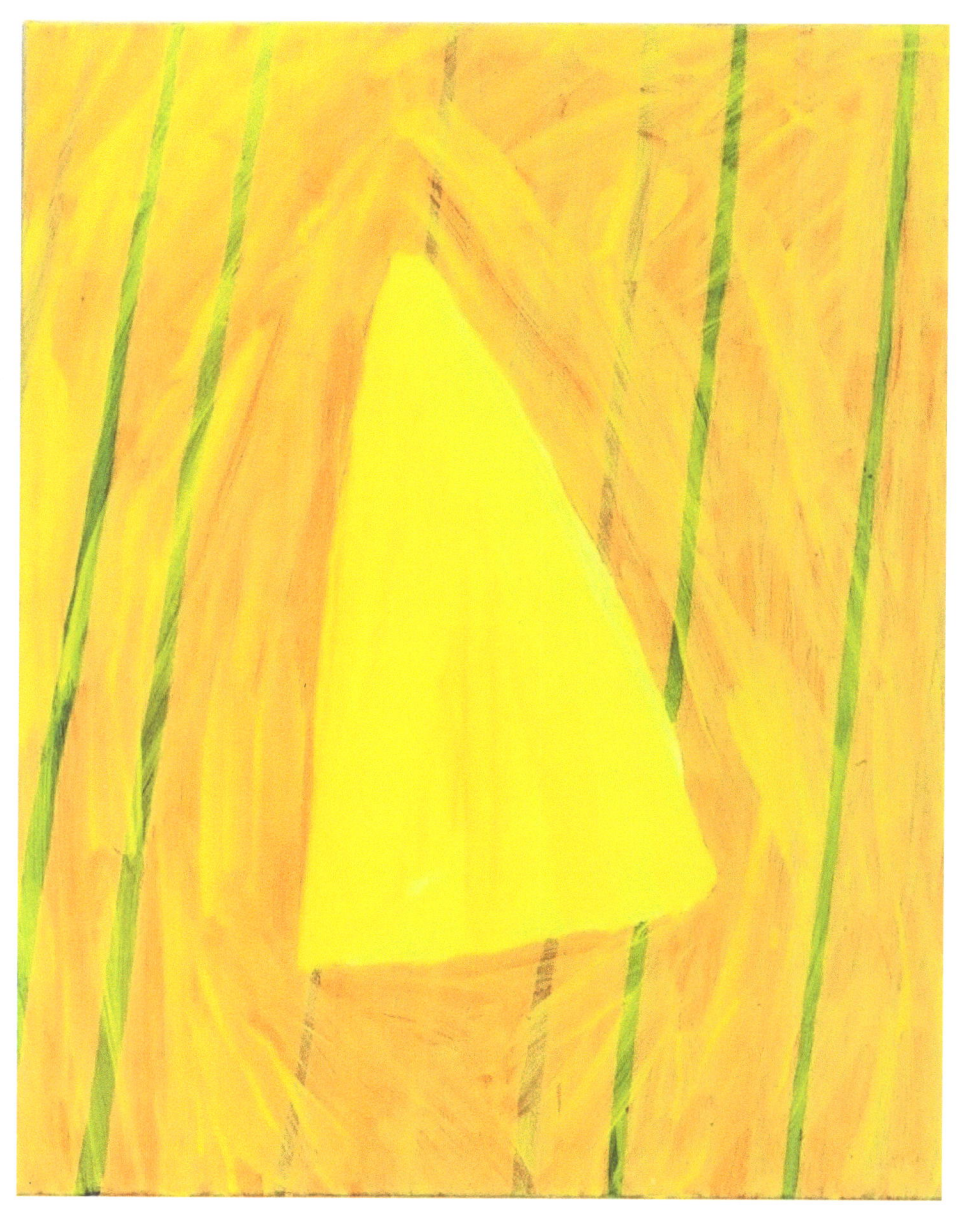

Untitled, acrylic on canvas, 20 x 16 inches, 2012

Jason Rohlf

Jason (b. 1970, Milwaukee, Wisconsin) studied Fine Art at the University of Wisconsin Milwaukee. A father of two daughters he paints and resides in Brooklyn, New York, since 1999.

Jason has exhibited nationally and is included in various corporate collections. In 2011, his first public art work was installed for the *Arts for Transit* program of New York City's Metropolitan Transportation Authority (MTA), in the Rockaways (Mott Avenue train station, A line).

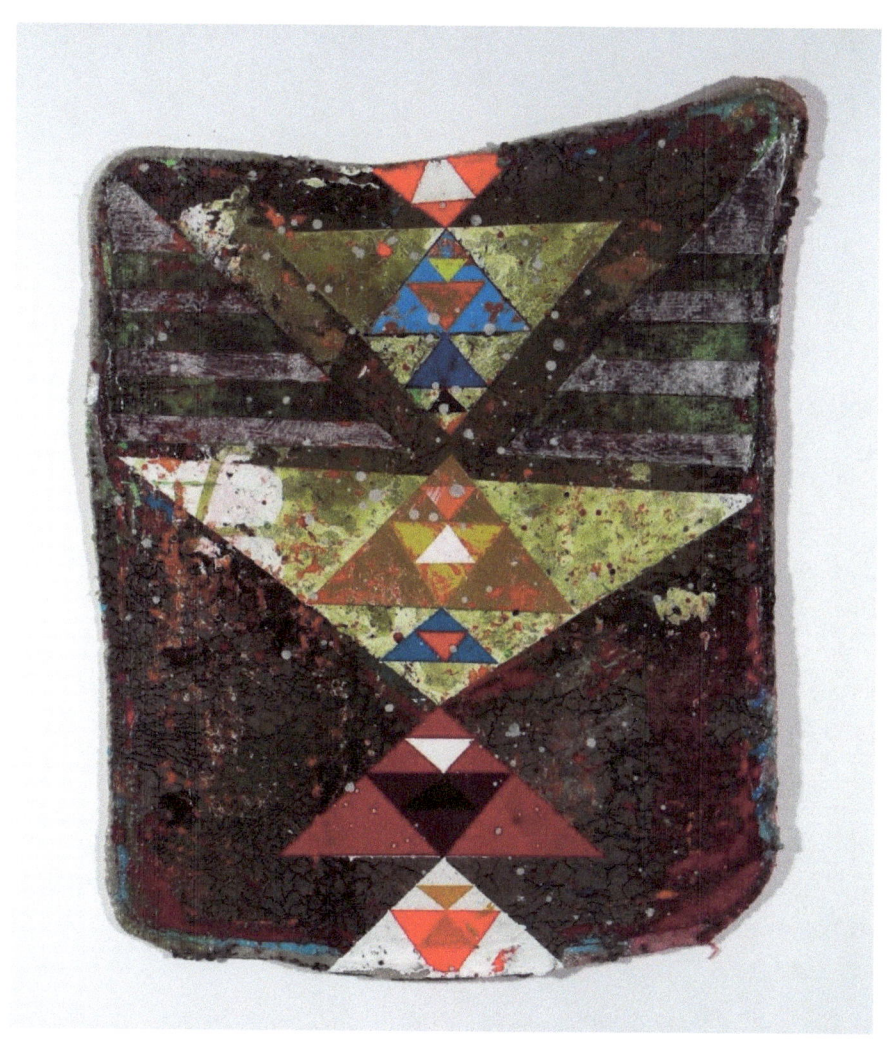

Stepped, acrylic/roof tar on shop rag, 17 x 13 inches, 2014

Li Trincere

Li Trincere (b. 1960, New York City) has exhibited her work internationally for the past 30 years, including in Australia, Belgium, Germany, New Zealand, Switzerland, and the United States.

During the early 1980s, she was heavily involved in the East Village abstract painting scene and showed at many of the landmark venues of the time, including Mission Gallery, Pyramid Club, Kamikaze Club, and The World. In the late 1980s and early 1990s, she exhibited at key galleries presenting new abstraction, such as Julian Pretto / Berland Hall, Stark Gallery, and Gabriele Bryers Gallery (all New York City), as well as the legendary Galerie Rolf Ricke in Cologne, Germany.

Trincere has received awards from the National Endowments for the Arts, Pollock-Krasner Foundation, Edward Albee Foundation, New York State Council on the Arts, and Artists Space. Her work has been reviewed in *The New York Times, Bomb Magazine, The Brooklyn Rail,* and *Kunstforum*, among others.

She holds an Master of Fine Arts in Painting from Hunter College, New York City, and a Bachelor of Fine Arts in Printmaking from Southampton College, Southampton, New York. She is represented by MINUS SPACE.

Untitled, acrylic on canvas, 60 x 18 inches, 2014

Julie Weitz

Julie Weitz is a visual artist based in Los Angeles, California. In her videos, paintings and drawings she renders a contemporary portrait of the Self, trapped between representation and abstraction, physical reality and virtual space, mind and body consciousness.

Weitz has exhibited widely and her work has been featured in prominent publications like the *New York Times, Art in America, Photograph Magazine* and *New American Paintings*. Recent solo shows include Agency (Los Angeles, California), The Suburban (Oak Park, Illinois), Mindy Solomon Gallery (St. Petersburg, Florida), William Busta Gallery (Cleveland, Ohio) and Tempus Projects (Tampa, Florida).

Weitz is a 2010 recipient of the West Prize for Emerging Artists. She has been awarded residencies at the 92nd St. Y, Oxbow, and 8550 OHIO. Weitz received her Bachelor of Fine Arts at University of Texas in Austin, and her Masters of Fine Arts at University of Wisconsin in Madison.

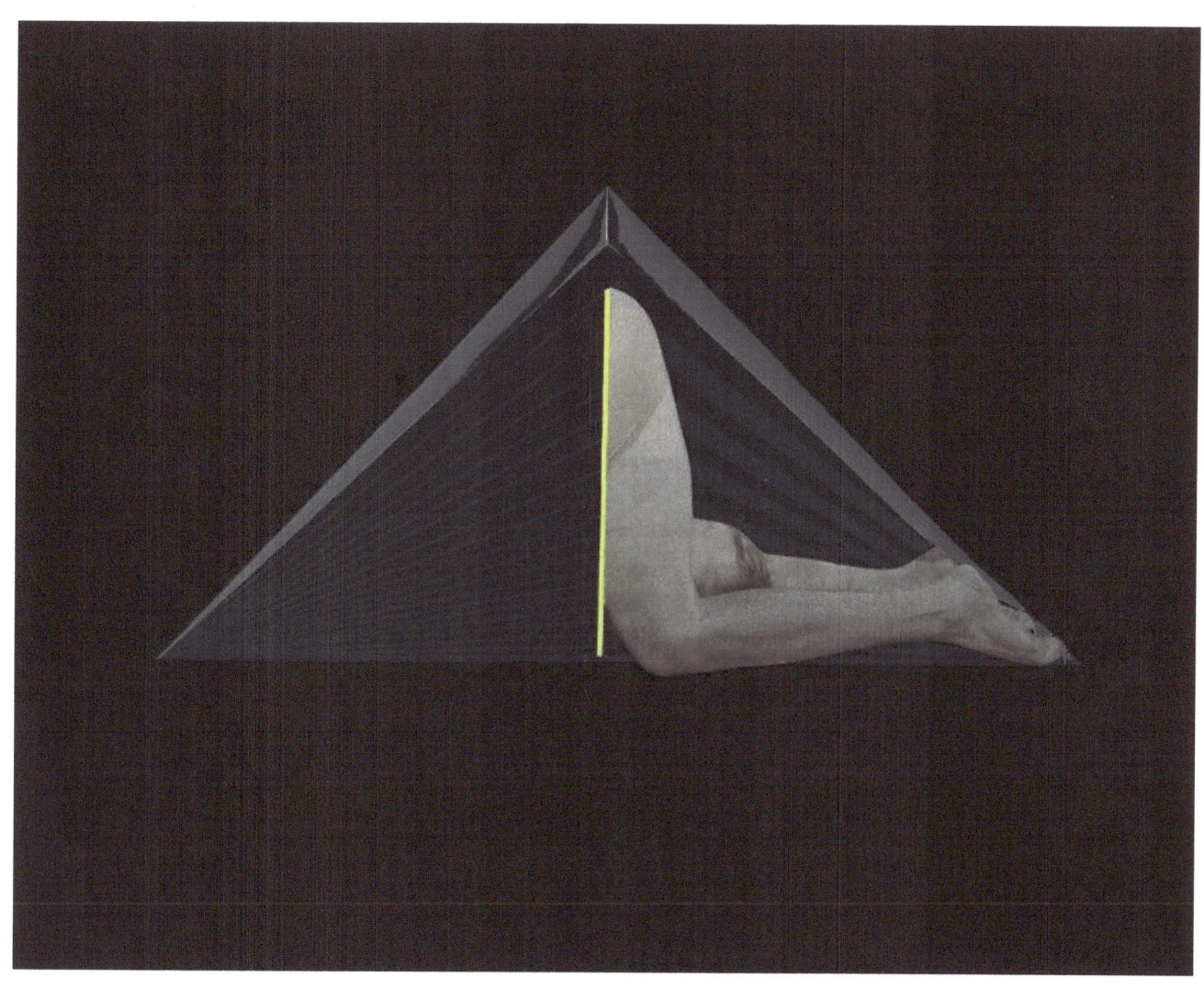

Shape No. 3, gouache, graphite ink mirror paper, tape and inkjet print, 9 x 12 inches, 2012

Thanks to the artists & writers,
Ana Busto and Steve Schiff of Ventana 244 Gallery, MINUS SPACE,
Janet Kurnatowski Gallery, Mindy Solomon Gallery & Stuber Publishing.

***

This catalog *Triangles* is available on Amazon.com – go to www.triangles.me/amazon